If we can stand up to [Hitler], all Europe may be free, and the life of the world may move forward into broad, sunlit uplands. But if we fail, then the whole world, including the United States, including all that we have known and cared for, will sink into the abyss of a new dark age. . .

Prime Minister of Great Britain
Winston Churchill, June 18, 1940

To the memory of my father, David Price, one of millions
of soldiers who fought against the Nazis

Photographs © 2010: akg-Images, London: 118 (RIA Novosti), 37, 85 top (ullstein bild), 18, 32; Alamy Images/
INTERFOTO: 50, 80 top; AP Images: 85 bottom (Sebastian Scheiner), 61, 80 center; Bridgeman Art Library
International Ltd., London/New York/Private Collection/Peter Newark Military Pictures: 45; Corbis Images:
84 bottom (Nathan Benn), 82 top, 83 center, 84 top, 85 center, 92, 100, 112, 129 (Bettmann); Getty Images: 124
(Laski Diffusion), 58 (FPG), 110 (Galerie Bilderwelt), 47, 66, 76, 80 bottom, 81 center left (Hulton Archive), 13 (H.
Miller), 23 (Popperfoto), 34 (Three Lions), 125 (William Vandivert/Time Life Pictures); Magnum Photos/Bar Am
Collection: 113; NEWSCOM: 30; The Granger Collection, New York: 83 top (ullstein bild), 89; The Image Works:
39 (Mary Evans Picture Library), 95 (The Jewish Chronicle Archive/HIP), 52 (Topfoto), 82 center, 115 (Topham);
United States Holocaust Memorial Museum: 84 center (Courtesy of Donald S. Robinson), 82 bottom (Courtesy
of Library of Congress), 71, 81 bottom, 81 top, 83 bottom, 106 (Courtesy of National Archives and Records
Administration, College Park), 81 center right (Courtesy of Shneur Elgar), 97 (Courtesy of Zydowski Instytut
Historyczny imienia Emanuela Ringelbluma).

Illustrations by XNR Productions, Inc.: 4, 5, 8, 9
Cover art, page 8 inset by Mark Summers
Chapter art by Raphael Montoliu

Library of Congress Cataloging-in-Publication Data
Price, Sean.
Adolf Hitler / Sean Stewart Price.
p. cm. — (A wicked history)
Includes bibliographical references and index.
ISBN-13: 978-0-531-20757-4 (lib. bdg.) 978-0-531-22357-4 (pbk.)
ISBN-10: 0-531-20757-9 (lib. bdg.) 0-531-22357-4 (pbk.)
1. Hitler, Adolf, 1889–1945—Juvenile literature. 2. Heads of
state—Germany—Biography—Juvenile literature. 3.
Germany—History—1933–1945—Juvenile literature. 4. National
socialism—Juvenile literature. I. Title.
DD247.H5P75 2010
943.086092—dc22
[B]
2009038734

Tod Olson, Series Editor
Marie O'Neill, Art Director
Allicette Torres, Cover Design
SimonSays Design!, Book Design and Production
Thanks to David Brandenberger, University of Richmond

© 2010 Scholastic Inc.

1 2 3 4 5 6 7 8 9 10 R 19 18 17 16 15 14 13 12 11 10   23

A WICKED HISTORY™
20TH CENTURY

Adolf Hitler

SEAN STEWART PRICE

Franklin Watts®
An Imprint of Scholastic Inc.
New York Toronto London Auckland Sydney
Mexico City New Delhi Hong Kong
Danbury, Connecticut

The World of
ADOLF HITLER

Hitler came to power in Germany in 1933 and then imposed his racist vision on nearly all of Europe during World War II.

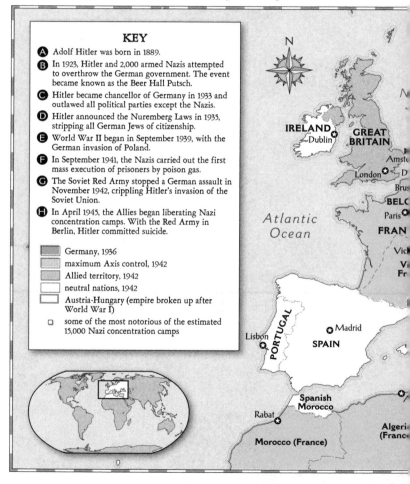

KEY

A Adolf Hitler was born in 1889.

B In 1923, Hitler and 2,000 armed Nazis attempted to overthrow the German government. The event became known as the Beer Hall Putsch.

C Hitler became chancellor of Germany in 1933 and outlawed all political parties except the Nazis.

D Hitler announced the Nuremberg Laws in 1935, stripping all German Jews of citizenship.

E World War II began in September 1939, with the German invasion of Poland.

F In September 1941, the Nazis carried out the first mass execution of prisoners by poison gas.

G The Soviet Red Army stopped a German assault in November 1942, crippling Hitler's invasion of the Soviet Union.

H In April 1945, the Allies began liberating Nazi concentration camps. With the Red Army in Berlin, Hitler committed suicide.

- Germany, 1936
- maximum Axis control, 1942
- Allied territory, 1942
- neutral nations, 1942
- Austria-Hungary (empire broken up after World War I)
- ▫ some of the most notorious of the estimated 15,000 Nazi concentration camps

TABLE OF CONTENTS

A Wicked Web

A look at the allies and enemies of Adolf Hitler.

Hitler's Family

∽∽∽∽∽∽∽∽∽∽∽∽∽∽

ALOIS HITLER
his father

KLARA HITLER
his mother

EVA BRAUN
his longtime girlfriend;
later his wife

Nazi Leaders

∽∽∽∽∽∽∽∽∽∽∽∽

HEINRICH HIMMLER
head of the Nazi Party's
military guard, the SS

REINHARD HEYDRICH
Himmler's
second-in-command

ERNST RÖHM
head of the Nazi
Storm Detachment, the SA

JOSEPH GOEBBELS
Nazi propaganda
minister

ADOLF HITLER

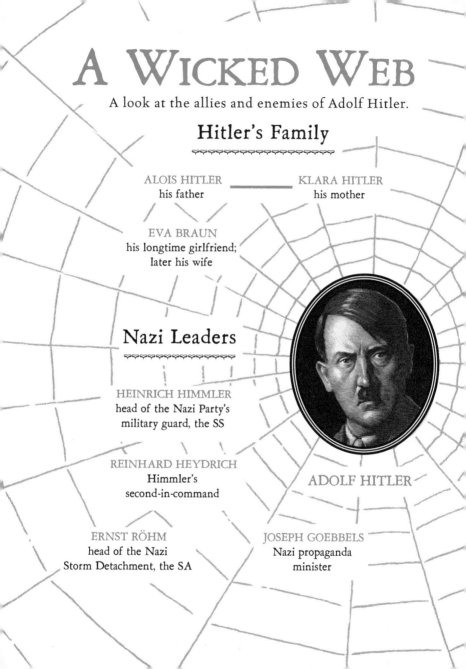

World Leaders

〜〜〜〜〜〜〜〜〜〜〜〜〜〜

BENITO MUSSOLINI
leader of Italy, 1922–1943

KURT SCHUSCHNIGG
chancellor of Austria,
1934–1938

NEVILLE CHAMBERLAIN
prime minister of Great Britain,
1937–1940

ÉDOUARD DALADIER
prime minister of France in
1933, 1934, and 1938–1940

FRANKLIN D. ROOSEVELT
president of the United States,
1933–1945

JOSEPH STALIN
leader of the Soviet Union,
1925–1953

WINSTON CHURCHILL
prime minister of Great Britain,
1940–1945 and 1951–1955

EDWARD R. MURROW THOUGHT HE HAD
seen it all. He had spent five and a half years reporting
on World War II for radio listeners in the United States.
He had seen cities shattered by bombs and roads lined
with dead soldiers. But nothing could have prepared
him for the horrors of Buchenwald.

During the final days of the war, Murrow was
following U.S. soldiers through Nazi Germany when
they discovered evidence of history's most notorious
crime. Behind a ring of barbed wire lay Buchenwald,
part of a vast system of concentration camps that
imprisoned the Nazi regime's victims. Inside the gates of
these camps, Nazi guards had systematically murdered
approximately six million Jews—a tragedy known
today as the Holocaust.

At least five million additional victims were
slaughtered in the camps, including Roma, gays,

Jehovah's Witnesses, political prisoners, prisoners of war, and others considered to be enemies of the Nazis.

As Murrow entered the camp's main gate, starving inmates crowded around him. "Men and boys reached out to touch me; they were in rags and remnants of uniforms," Murrow reported in his radio broadcast. "Death had already marked many of them." Some would die of disease or starvation later that day.

Murrow asked a survivor to show him around the camp. Signs of unimaginable suffering were everywhere. Inmates had been shot, beaten, whipped, and hanged. Others had been starved and worked to death. The barracks reeked of dead bodies and excrement. Starving children milled around, their ribs visible through their thin shirts. In a courtyard, Murrow saw two piles of dead bodies—several hundred naked men and boys stacked up "like cordwood."

Shortly after the liberation of Buchenwald, someone hung a life-sized figure from one of the camp's gallows. The figure was made to look like Adolf Hitler, Nazi

Germany's supreme leader, or *führer*. The figure swung by its neck in a cool spring breeze. Behind it was a message scrawled in white paint: "Hitler must die for Germany to live."

Few people could argue with the sentiment. Adolf Hitler had ruled Germany with an iron fist since 1933. He had risen to power behind a deadly philosophy of revenge and racial hatred. His orders had created Buchenwald and the other camps and filled them with victims. His dreams of conquest had triggered the worldwide war that U.S. soldiers and their allies were still racing to finish.

As Murrow completed his grisly tour, Hitler was ranting and raving through the final days of his life. But the devastation the dictator had unleashed would last for generations and leave millions of people struggling to comprehend its scope.

Murrow ended his radio broadcast on Buchenwald with these thoughts: "I pray you to believe what I have said about Buchenwald. I reported what I saw and heard, but only part of it. For most of it, I have no words."

SURVIVORS of Buchenwald on April 16, 1945, five days after the death camp was liberated by U.S. troops. Among them is 16-year-old Elie Wiesel (second bunk, seventh from left), who later wrote *Night*, a memoir of his horrifying experiences in Nazi concentration camps.

PART 1

ROOTS OF HATRED

CHAPTER 1

An Angry Youth

Hitler acquires some DANGEROUS IDEAS.

ADOLF HITLER WAS BORN ON APRIL 20, 1889. Although he would come to dominate Germany, he was born in Austria-Hungary, an empire on Germany's eastern and southern borders.

Adolf was raised in a small town called Braunau am Inn. His mother, Klara, doted on him from the start. She had already lost three children to disease and was desperate for her fourth to survive. Hitler would later boast that he was his "mother's darling."

Adolf's childhood was dominated by conflict with his father. Alois Hitler worked as a customs officer, inspecting goods traveling in and out of Austria. He wanted Adolf to follow in his footsteps and work for the government. The idea revolted Adolf. Their feud continued until Alois died suddenly in 1903.

By age 15, Adolf was failing several subjects in school. His teachers were fed up with him. One teacher described him as "obstinate" and "hot-tempered."

Hitler hated all his teachers except one. Dr. Leonard Poetsch was a fierce German nationalist. At the time, parts of Austria-Hungary were dominated by German-speaking people. Poetsch argued that these areas should all be united with Germany.

Poetsch taught Hitler about Otto von Bismarck, the German chancellor who was famous for starting, and winning, several wars. "The great issues of the day will be decided not by means of speeches and majority resolutions," he had once said, "but by iron and blood!"

This was a lesson that Hitler would not forget.

GERMAN NATIONALISM

JUST TWO DECADES BEFORE HITLER WAS BORN, Germany did not exist as a nation. German-speaking people lived in 39 small and independent states in central Europe. But many Germans believed that if they formed a single, unified country, they would be powerful enough to dominate the rest of Europe.

Those people, known as German nationalists, got their way in 1871. The skilled statesman Otto von Bismarck brought 40 million Germans together into the new German Empire.

But despite Bismarck's efforts, millions of German-speakers still lived in the diverse empire of Austria-Hungary. Many of these ethnic Germans—like Hitler's teacher Dr. Poetsch—believed that all Germans should live together in a single nation. Many also came to believe in the myth that ethnic Germans were racially superior to the other peoples of the world. As he grew up, Adolf Hitler became a fanatical convert to the German nationalist cause.

OTTO VON
BISMARCK

CHAPTER 2

Dropout

Hitler quits school and spends five
years DOWN AND OUT IN VIENNA.

AT AGE 16, ADOLF HITLER DROPPED OUT
of school. He spent the next two years at home, drawing,
going to the opera, and idling away the days. It was, he
later claimed, the happiest time of his life. But it all came
to an end in December 1907, when Klara Hitler died of
breast cancer.

Hitler then moved to Vienna, Austria, where he
could chase a dream of becoming a great artist. He applied
to study at the city's Academy of Fine Arts. The art

school rejected him and he flew into a rage. "The whole Academy ought to be blown up!" he ranted to a friend.

By the fall of 1909, Hitler had run through the money his mother had left him. He abandoned his apartment. He lost weight, and his hair and beard grew shaggy. By day, he prowled the streets. At night, he'd sleep at a homeless shelter, or in a park or doorway.

Still, Hitler refused to get a regular job. He made a meager living selling his paintings. But his favorite pastime was to argue politics. He typically ended arguments by calling his rivals "idiots."

In Vienna, Hitler found a target for his restless anger. The city had a large and thriving Jewish population. Jewish merchants and business owners were major contributors to the city's booming economy. More than half of Vienna's doctors and lawyers were Jewish. And the Jewish community had produced many world-famous musicians and writers.

But for centuries, Jews had been treated with envy and suspicion in the cities of Europe—and Vienna was no exception. A wave of anti-Semitism, or hatred of Jews, spread through the city. Popular magazines claimed that Jews were taking over Vienna. The mayor accused Jewish bankers of controlling Vienna's economy.

Hitler fell right into step with the city's anti-Semites. He blamed Jewish residents for the city's crime rate. He complained that Jews controlled the art and music worlds. "Wherever I went, I now saw Jews," Hitler later wrote in his autobiography, "and the more I saw, the more sharply they set themselves apart in my eyes from the rest of humanity."

Hitler would later call Vienna "the hardest, most thorough school of my life." By May 1913, he had decided to leave for good. Packing his one small, battered bag, he moved to the city of Munich, Germany. Hitler wanted to live somewhere he considered thoroughly German, and he was not disappointed. "The city itself was as familiar to me as if I had lived for years within its walls," he later wrote.

C H A P T E R   3

A Soldier's Life

Hitler finds a PURPOSE IN LIFE—
in the trenches of World War I.

CHEERS ROSE FROM THE STREETS OF Munich. On August 2, 1914, thousands of Germans jammed the city's central square to celebrate the beginning of World War I. Twenty-five-year-old Adolf Hitler joined the happy throng.

A month earlier, an assassin had shot and killed the heir to the empire of Austria-Hungary. The murder ignited long-smoldering hostilities across the continent. One after another, the great powers of Europe chose sides and went to war. On one side were the Central Powers, which included Germany, Austria-Hungary, and the Ottoman Empire. They faced the Triple Entente, also known as the Allies: Great Britain, France, and Russia. (The United States would later join the Allies.)

Hitler immediately volunteered for the German army. As a German nationalist, he threw himself into

A CHEERING CROWD gathers in Munich on August 2, 1914, one day after Germany's declaration of war. Adolf Hitler (circled) was part of the celebration.

his new task with fanatic devotion. "I sank down upon my knees and thanked Heaven," he later wrote.

On August 16, as the German army crashed across the border into Belgium and France, Hitler reported for duty in Munich. Over the next four years, he would participate in dozens of brutal trench battles along the border with France. The regiment he fought with lost 3,754 men. Yet Hitler somehow survived.

The fighting ended for Hitler on the night of October 13, 1918, when he was temporarily blinded by a poison gas attack. While he was recovering, a pastor tearfully informed him that Germany had lost the war. Angry sailors, soldiers, and workers were rioting in the streets and had forced the emperor to step down. The moderate Social Democratic Party had taken over, calling for democracy and workers' rights. On November 11, the new government signed an armistice to end the fighting. By the end of the month, Germany's defeated ally, the empire of Austria-Hungary, had been broken up into separate countries.

After hearing the news, Hitler spent many sleepless nights stewing over Germany's defeat. Like many angry Germans, he told himself that Germany never should have surrendered. "Only fools, liars, and criminals could hope in the mercy of the enemy," he wrote. "In these nights hatred grew in me, hatred for those responsible for this deed."

Hitler blamed the defeat on a group he called the "November criminals." He considered the Social Democrats to be the main offenders. But his rage wasn't just directed at a political party; it had grown deeper and more ominous than that.

Anti-Semitism had begun to color Hitler's entire view of the world. He was convinced that the Social Democratic Party was controlled by Jews. Jewish bankers, he charged, had failed to support the war effort. In his bitter imagination, the German surrender was part of a vast Jewish conspiracy to weaken the German state and seize control of its government.

Hitler's explanation for Germany's defeat was, in

fact, paranoid and incorrect. By the time the Social Democrats took power, the German economy had reached a breaking point. Millions of Germans suffered from unemployment and food shortages. The economic crisis would have forced the Germans to negotiate for peace no matter who controlled the government.

The so-called "Jewish conspiracy" was just as much a product of Hitler's imagination. During four years of warfare, German Jews had proved their patriotism. Jews were better represented in the German military than any other ethnic or religious group. Nearly 12,000 Jews had died in the trenches by the end of the war.

The facts, however, did not matter to Hitler. His hatred was all-consuming, and it focused his mind on the future. The "November criminals," he insisted, had forced surrender on Germany. Now he wanted to make them pay. He vowed to get rid of them all—the Social Democrats, the Jews, the peace-lovers. In his vindictive imagination, he began to think that he would be the man to raise Germany up from defeat.

CHAPTER 4

Nazi Menace

Hitler takes control of the Nazi
Party and SPREADS HATRED
in the beer halls of Munich.

Hitler EMERGED FROM THE HOSPITAL TO
find that Germany had descended into chaos. After
four years of war, the economy was a mess. The
new democratic government, known as the Weimar
Republic, faced fierce opposition from both communists
and conservatives.

Communist groups accused the party in power, the
Social Democrats, of ignoring the needs of struggling
workers. The communists wanted to seize control of

Germany in a violent revolution, place all businesses under government control, and distribute wealth equally among the people.

Conservatives hated the communists and the Social Democrats. They accused both groups of treason for their role in surrendering to the Allies. They wanted to stamp out democracy and bring back the emperor. Only then, they insisted, would the Germans regain the strength and honor they had lost during the war.

The communists and the conservatives fought zealously to impose their vision on Germany. Groups from both sides formed private armies and sent them to battle each other in the streets.

In June 1919, the victors in World War I gave the German people another reason to protest. Led by France, the Allies forced the new German government to sign a harsh peace agreement called the Treaty of Versailles. As a result, Germany was stripped of 13 percent of its territory and was fined more than $30 billion. The treaty also severely limited the size of the German military.

Ex-soldiers like Hitler reacted to the treaty with anger and disbelief. They had marched off to fight for one of the world's strongest, most stable monarchies. Now they returned home to find a weak, floundering democracy. Many Germans felt betrayed—"stabbed in the back," as Hitler wrote.

In September 1919, Hitler's resentment led him to one of the many new political parties formed after the war. After settling in Munich, he began attending meetings of a tiny nationalist group. It would soon take the name National Socialist German Worker's Party (or Nazi Party). Hitler had wanted to start his own party. But here was a small organization that he could shape however he chose.

Hitler began giving speeches in taverns and meeting halls in and around Munich. He drew crowds of one or two hundred at first—and put on a fiery show. He used his hands restlessly, stabbing the air with his finger or clenching his fist to make a point.

The effect was mesmerizing—and the message was ominous. Hitler railed against the "November

HITLER COMMANDED attention from his audiences with loud outbursts and fiery gestures. He developed his speaking style by practicing to recordings of his speeches. Photos like this one, from 1925, were taken so he could study his technique.

criminals" he blamed for crippling Germany. He spewed hatred against Jews and communists. In his view, all Jews should be barred from public office— and deported if there weren't enough jobs to go around. He urged Germans to use force to seize the government from the Social Democrats. "The misery of Germany must be broken by Germany's steel," he declared. "That time must come."

Hitler prepared for this revolution by recruiting ex-soldiers into a growing army of thugs. His

"Brownshirts"—named for their uniforms—became a menacing presence in the Munich area. They roamed the streets in small gangs and often beat up Jews who crossed their paths. They came to Nazi Party meetings and brutalized hecklers with riding whips and hard rubber clubs. Sometimes Hitler sent them into rival party meetings to intimidate speakers and start brawls. The communists had their own private militias, which fought with equal ferocity.

Hitler encouraged violence at every turn. In the fall of 1921, he turned his Brownshirts into an organization known as the Storm Detachment, or SA. "The [Nazi Party] has been described as a savage, brutal horde," he said in November 1921. "I am very happy to hear this since I expect that this will make my aims and my party feared and known."

Hitler's party also got help from the German economy, which continued to decline after the war. The government was forced to print massive amounts of money in order to pay its fines to the Allies. Prices soared, making it hard for ordinary Germans to put food on the table. Savings became worthless overnight. Workers had to be paid twice a day because their wages lost value so quickly.

Millions of Germans were out of work, and the Nazi Party appealed to both their fears and their hopes.

BY 1923, THE GERMAN ECONOMY had collapsed. It took a wheelbarrow full of money just to buy a loaf of bread. Here, men carry baskets full of cash into a bank in Berlin.

Hitler's angry tirades against Jews and communists gave struggling workers someone to blame for their problems. His pledge to make Germany strong again made people feel like they could look forward to a brighter future. By late 1923, more than 20,000 Germans had sworn allegiance to the Nazi cause.

Hitler decided that the time was ripe to seize power. He launched a *putsch*, or government takeover, by kidnapping three high government officials while they attended a rally at a Munich beer hall. Shortly after 8:30 P.M. on November 8, 1923, Hitler mounted a podium in the beer hall and fired a pistol in the air. The gunshot stunned and silenced the crowd of about 3,000. "The national revolution has begun!" Hitler declared.

The next day, he led about 2,000 Nazis into the streets of Munich. Hitler assumed that the army and ordinary Germans would flock to his cause, march on the capital of Berlin, and seize control of the government. In fact, both the army and the German people did nothing as the state police mobilized against

NAZI BROWNSHIRTS in Munich, Germany, during the Beer Hall Putsch. Hitler was arrested for treason after his failed attempt to overthrow the German government.

Hitler's rabble. Shortly after noon, the police opened fire on the Nazis. At least 21 people were killed, and the Nazis scattered.

Hitler tried to go into hiding, but the police tracked him down and arrested him for high treason. His political career appeared to have come to an end.

CHAPTER 5

Mein Kampf

Hitler is convicted of TREASON.

AFTER THE BEER HALL PUTSCH, HITLER was charged with treason and thrown into a prison near Munich. The once-proud Nazi leader had become a laughingstock in Germany. Political cartoons made fun of the man who tried to launch a putsch from a beer hall.

But the people who failed to take Hitler seriously were making a dangerous mistake. In February 1924, Hitler went on trial, and he seized control of the proceedings. Before a huge crowd of journalists and cheering supporters, he turned the courtroom into a theater for Nazi propaganda. He yelled at the judges and the witnesses. His opening comments alone lasted four hours.

Hitler stood before his accusers and admitted that he was guilty of launching the putsch. But he insisted that the real criminals were the men who had surrendered to the Allies and signed the Treaty of Versailles. "There is no such thing as high treason against the traitors of 1918!" he thundered. By his closing speech, Hitler had reporters weeping in sympathy.

Hitler's judges gave him the minimum sentence— five years. But his special treatment did not end there. At Landsberg Prison, guards allowed a constant stream of visitors. Friends brought news from the outside world, as well as home-cooked food that Hitler ate in his comfortably furnished cell.

The most important gift Hitler received came from the warden at Landsberg. It was a typewriter, and over the next nine months, Hitler sat in his cell and wrote his autobiography. He titled it *Mein Kampf*, or "My Struggle." In 782 rambling pages, Hitler laid out his plans for the future of Germany. At the heart of his book lay a viciously racist view of human life.

Hitler claimed that all of humanity was divided into "superior" and "inferior" races. The "Aryan," or northern European, race, he said, occupied the top rank. The ideal Aryan, according to Hitler, had blond hair and blue eyes. Near the bottom of Hitler's ladder stood Africans, Asians, Slavs, and others. As always, he assigned the lowest position to Jews.

Today, scientists believe there is no basis for classifying people by race, much less claiming that one group is inferior to another.

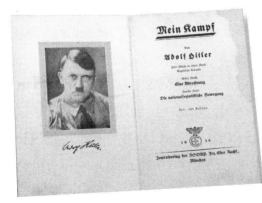

HITLER WROTE *Mein Kampf* while in prison for treason. In it, he laid out his racist vision of the future. He argued that the so-called Aryan race of northern Europe must dominate the world by sheer force.

Hitler further insisted that the future of Germany—and in fact of all humanity—would be determined by a struggle between the races. The Aryan race, he urged, had to take up the challenge and defeat its weaker rivals. "The stronger must dominate, and not blend with the weaker, thus sacrificing his own greatness," he wrote.

There was no room for democracy in Hitler's brutal worldview. The common people should be ruled by the elite, he insisted. Members of groups he considered inferior, he said, should not be allowed to vote.

There was also little room for peace. The Aryan race needed *lebensraum*, or "living space," in order to expand and thrive, Hitler claimed. And he insisted that so-called superior races had a right—even a duty—to seize land from races deemed to be inferior. Hitler made no attempt to disguise his ruthless intentions. He wanted to invade Poland and the Soviet Union. He would then expel or enslave all Slavs and Jews, and send Germans to colonize the conquered land.

As he finished his manuscript, Hitler began to consider his plans for rebuilding the Nazi Party. Before the Beer Hall Putsch, his intent had been to seize power at the point of a gun. Now he decided to take control of Germany legally, through democratic elections.

Hitler left prison on a raw December day in 1924, freed after just nine months for "good behavior." Two associates met him at the gates and drove him to Munich. One of the associates asked Hitler what he planned to do now that he was free. "I shall start again," he said, "from the beginning."

HITLER STANDS outside Landsberg Prison on the day of his release. Hitler was now determined to take power in Germany through legal elections.

PART 2

A BLOODY RISE TO POWER

Chapter 6

Starting Over

Hitler revives the Nazi Party and GAINS CONTROL OF GERMANY.

WHEN HITLER LEFT PRISON, HE FOUND that Germany had made a strong recovery since his arrest. The government had reversed the terrible rise in prices. Foreign loans from the United States helped pump up the German economy. People had jobs. The future finally looked bright for the German people.

The booming economy made it harder for the Nazis to sell their message of hate. Hitler relied on anger and outrage to win supporters. Happy, prosperous Germans had little need for his conspiracy theories. In the 1924 elections to the German parliament, known as the Reichstag, National Socialists won just three percent of the vote.

Deprived of power in the Reichstag, Hitler used the next few years to build and strengthen the Nazi Party. He appointed regional party leaders to enforce his orders and trained public speakers to spread the Nazi message. The party was small. But its 40,000 members were fanatically devoted to their cause and ready to take advantage of their next opportunity.

That opportunity came in the form of the devastating economic crisis known as the Great Depression. On October 24, 1929, the U.S. stock market crashed. Banks failed all around the world, shattering the economies of wealthy countries like the United States, Great Britain, and France. Germany's foreign loans dried up. Most business activity collapsed. Unemployment in Germany jumped from 650,000 people before the crash to more than five million in the early 1930s.

The Social Democrats, who still ruled Germany, watched their support fade away. Millions of Germans had lost everything and blamed the government for their misery. Many people began to think that the communists or the Nazis might offer them a better life. In the 1930 elections, the Nazi Party won 18.3 percent of the vote. That made it the second-largest party in the Reichstag after the Social Democrats.

For several years, Adolf Hitler had been the führer, or supreme leader, of a party that had very little real political power. Now, almost overnight, he had become one of Germany's most influential politicians.

Power lay within Hitler's grasp. But to many Germans, the Nazis were still little more than a group of brown-shirted thugs. Hitler worked relentlessly to make the Nazis appear respectable. After the Beer Hall Putsch, local governments across Germany had banned the SA from appearing publicly in uniform. Hitler urged his Brownshirts to obey the laws and to stop assaulting communists and Jews in the streets.

Hitler also gave dozens of public speeches, carefully tailoring his message to each audience. When he spoke to business people, he criticized labor unions. To labor groups, he promised to create jobs. Before intellectuals, he downplayed his plans to persecute Jews. To many people, Hitler seemed to be a fairly reasonable man who just wanted to restore Germany to greatness.

Hitler relied on his propaganda minister, Joseph Goebbels, to spread his message. Goebbels printed posters with a slogan calling for Germans to unify behind Hitler: "One People, One Country, One Führer." The posters, along with the Nazi swastika flag, began to appear in every open space. Goebbels also introduced "*Heil* Hitler!" (Hail Hitler!) as the Nazi greeting.

A NAZI PROPAGANDA POSTER calls for Germans to "wake up!"

To many Germans, battered by hard times, the Nazis began to seem young, vibrant, and energetic. One young party member remembered seeing swastikas painted on the sidewalks and Nazi pamphlets blanketing the streets. "There was a feeling of restless energy about [the Nazis]," she recalled. "I was drawn by the feeling of strength about the party, even though there was much in it that was highly questionable."

The popularity of the Nazis drew thousands of new recruits to the SA. Even though they were banned by law, Hitler's private army of Brownshirts grew to 400,000 members by the spring of 1932. Their commander, an ex-soldier named Ernst Röhm, itched to turn his thugs loose.

In June 1932, Hitler got the ban on the SA lifted. The Brownshirts once again took to the streets armed with clubs and guns. They beat up Jews and disrupted communist rallies. The communists sent their own thugs to do battle with the SA, and in July alone 86 people were killed in riots.

The Nazis were issuing a threat: Give us power or we will take it at the point of a gun. On July 31, voters gave the Nazi Party more seats in the Reichstag than any other single party.

Hitler's moment had finally arrived. Germany's moderate leaders feared the growing power of the communists more than they feared the Nazis. So a small group of politicians convinced President Paul von

SUPPORTERS GREET Hitler in Nuremberg. On January 30, 1933, he was named chancellor—the head of Germany's government.

Hindenburg to appoint Hitler chancellor. On January 30, 1933, Hitler became—along with Hindenburg—one of the two most powerful men in the German government.

That night, Hitler stood at a reviewing stand in Berlin while triumphant Brownshirts paraded past carrying torches and singing Nazi anthems. The Nazi führer would still have to share power with President Hindenburg. But Hitler now had real control over the laws and policies of the entire country.

As the Nazis celebrated, at least one German had an insight into the future. General Erich Ludendorff, the army's second-in-command during World War I, was shocked that Hindenburg had put Hitler in charge of the country. "I solemnly prophesy that this accursed man will cast [Germany] into the abyss and bring our nation to inconceivable misery," Ludendorff told the president. "Future generations will damn you in your grave for what you have done."

CHAPTER 7

Up in Flames

With the reins of power finally in his hands, Hitler STAMPS OUT DEMOCRACY in Germany.

ON THE NIGHT OF FEBRUARY 27, 1933, a deep red glow appeared in the Berlin sky. Sparks and flames rose into the air. Berliners gathered in the street and watched a massive fire devour the Reichstag building, home of Germany's democratically elected parliament.

To some in the crowd, the fire seemed deeply symbolic: Less than a month after the Nazis took power, the seat of German democracy had been destroyed.

THE REICHSTAG—home of the German parliament—goes up in flames. Hitler blamed the fire on the communists and used it as an excuse to turn Germany into a police state.

To this day, many people suspect that the Nazis planned the Reichstag fire. But Hitler immediately declared that the fire was a vicious act of terrorism planned and carried out by the communists. As he walked through the charred ruins of the Reichstag, he insisted it was just the beginning of a communist revolution. "This is a God-given signal," he exclaimed. "We must crush this murderous pest with an iron fist!"

Using the communist threat as his excuse, Hitler began to crack down on all opposition to Nazi rule. The day after the fire, he steamrolled President Hindenburg into issuing a decree for the "Protection of the People and State." The decree destroyed civil liberties in Germany. It suspended freedom of speech and the right to assemble in public. Newspapers could now be censored by the government. Rival political parties were banned from holding rallies. Anyone who criticized the government could be thrown in jail.

Hitler used his Brownshirts to enforce the decree. SA thugs raided communist offices and destroyed printing presses. They seized 25,000 communists and Social Democrats and threw them in jail. According to Christopher Isherwood, a British writer living in Berlin,

A SOLDIER FROM the Nazi Party's private army, the SA, holds German communists at gunpoint. Members of the SA were called Brownshirts, and by 1933, they numbered more than three million. After the Reichstag fire, the SA rounded up at least 25,000 of Hitler's political enemies.

Germany became a place of "illegal midnight arrests, of prisoners tortured in the SA barracks."

The prisoners arrested by the SA were tried before special courts. Those not killed outright were thrown into prison camps.

These camps were run by the SS, or *Schutzstaffel* (defense unit). Originally formed to guard Hitler, the SS quickly became one of his main tools of terror. He would also create the Gestapo, or State Secret Police, to hunt down political opponents.

On March 23, a month after the Reichstag fire, Hitler called a special session of the parliament and asked the lawmakers to pass a bill called the Enabling Act. The act would give Hitler the power to suspend the constitution and change any law. As the Reichstag members voted, a mob of Brownshirts chanted in the halls: "We want the bill—or fire and murder!"

The bill was passed into law by a vote of 441 to 94.

Now only two obstacles stood between Hitler and complete control of Germany's government—the army and President Hindenburg.

Hitler had an uneasy relationship with Germany's generals. Many of the veteran military leaders feared the strength of Hitler's zealous young Brownshirts. The SA had grown into a massive force of more than three million men. Their commander, Ernst Röhm, was hungry for power. Röhm wanted to merge the SA and the army and take command of the entire military force.

As Röhm pressed his demands, the generals began to insist that Hitler get rid of the SA commander. Hitler knew he had to choose between Röhm and the generals—and he chose the generals. The Brownshirts had paved the way for Hitler's rise to power, but they were not a disciplined fighting force. Hitler would need an experienced and loyal army to carry out his plans for foreign conquest in the years to come. Besides, Röhm's demands for more power had begun to make Hitler suspect that Röhm was planning a putsch of his own.

To protect his plans for the future, Hitler made a deal with the generals. He would remove Röhm in exchange for the army's support.

On June 30, 1934, Hitler struck. He launched a bloody rampage against the SA that became known as the "Night of the Long Knives."

Hitler accused Röhm of plotting to overthrow the government. Then he ordered loyal SS squads to round up SA leaders. Dozens of baffled Brownshirts were dragged out of their beds, lined up, and shot. Many were longtime party members who died giving the stiff-armed Nazi salute and shouting "Heil Hitler!"

Hitler himself flew to the Alps, where Röhm was vacationing. The führer barged into Röhm's bedroom, pistol in hand. He told Röhm curtly he was a traitor and then left him with armed guards. The SA leader could only sputter his innocence and demand that Hitler come back and talk. Röhm was taken to a nearby jail cell and shot. His dying words were "My führer, my führer."

Nearly 200 people were murdered during Hitler's purge of the SA. Some Germans were horrified by the gangster-style executions. Hitler expressed no remorse. In fact, he announced to the nation that he was now the "supreme judge of the German people." If anyone dared to plot against the German government, he warned, "then certain death is his lot."

Under a new commander, the Brownshirts remained an intimidating force in Germany. But with Röhm gone and the generals satisfied, Hitler had ensured the loyalty of both the SA and the army.

The last obstacle to Hitler's power fell about one month later, when President Hindenburg died. Hitler proclaimed himself "führer and chancellor." At age 45, Hitler had sole control of Germany and its 66 million people.

ᘐᘐᘐᘐᘐᘐᘐᘐᘐᘐᘐᘐᘐ

A Chilling Spectacle

Millions of Germans fall UNDER THE SPELL of the Nazis.

ON SEPTEMBER 7, 1934, 200,000 DEVOTED Nazis crowded onto Zeppelin Field outside the city of Nuremberg, Germany. Some 20,000 Nazi banners fluttered above the sea of black and brown shirts. Massive searchlights swept across the dark sky and the crowd. The glow could be seen 100 miles away.

For seven years, Nazis had been gathering at Nuremberg for the Nazi Party's annual rally. This year,

NAZIS STAND IN FORMATION at a rally in the 1930s. After Hitler took power, he began to introduce fascism into Germany. That's a system of government in which a dictator holds complete power, suppresses all dissent, and emphasizes nationalism, racism, and terror.

the event served as a massive, week-long celebration of their rise to power. Every day, the field was darkened by uniforms as Nazi soldiers lined up with military precision. Hitler addressed the crowd several times during the week. "We are strong and will get stronger!" he roared. When he finished, the entire crowd gave a stiff-armed salute, shouting "Heil Hitler!" and *"Sieg Heil!"* (Hail Victory!).

The Nuremberg rallies were giant propaganda shows. They were carefully designed to demonstrate the power of the Nazi Party and instill a fanatical devotion to the führer. But to outsiders who watched the proceedings on newsreels, the rallies were chilling spectacles—signs that an entire country was falling under the spell of a madman.

In less than two years, Hitler had rebuilt Germany around a political philosophy known as fascism. Fascists such as Hitler and the Italian dictator Benito Mussolini were fierce nationalists. They insisted that the nation was more important than the individual. In a fascist state, people had to give up their individual freedoms and devote themselves to a common purpose.

Fascists also rejected democracy. Free elections, they argued, destroyed the unity of the nation. The common people were thought to be too weak and ignorant to govern. In the fascist view of government, only a dictator who unified the masses could lead a nation to greatness.

In keeping with the fascist model, the Nazi Party extended its reach into all parts of German life. Germans no longer said *"guten tag"* (good day) to greet each other. They now said "Heil Hitler." Teachers used the phrase at the beginning of class. Business people opened meetings with it.

Hitler paid particular attention to young people, hoping to ensure their loyalty as they grew up. At 14, all German boys joined an organization called the Hitler Youth. Hitler Youth groups met regularly to study Nazi doctrine and hold rallies. Boys in the Hitler Youth did military drills and rigorous exercises. Their leaders encouraged brutality between students in order to train the boys for future service in the SA or SS.

YOUNG BOYS perform during a Hitler Youth parade. Hitler Youth were given racist history and biology texts and spent many hours every day in physical training.

Boys in the Hitler Youth were also taught the Nazis' racist theories. Children were urged not to socialize with Jews or other members of groups considered inferior by the Nazis.

By 1935, life had grown increasingly dangerous for German Jews. Nazi Brownshirts hung signs outside Jewish-owned stores that read, "Whoever buys from a Jew is a traitor to the people." Every month, laws were passed that cost thousands of Jewish citizens their jobs. In Munich, Jewish doctors were forbidden to treat non-Jewish patients. Racist laws barred Jewish accountants from consulting on taxes, Jewish actors from performing in public, and Jewish civilians from working in the military.

That September, at the annual Nazi rally, Hitler made an ominous announcement. Under a new set of laws, all German Jews would be deprived of their citizenship. They would also be banned from marrying non-Jews. The so-called Nuremberg Laws made it clear to anyone who may have doubted Hitler's intentions: Under the Nazis, German Jews were no longer welcome in their own country.

In fascist Germany, people who criticized Hitler's anti-Semitic laws—or any other Nazi policy—risked their freedom and even their lives. Gestapo agents seemed to be listening everywhere. Ordinary German civilians were expected to inform on their neighbors.

Hitler Youth denounced their own parents as traitors. Even telling a joke about Hitler or complaining about food prices could result in a visit from the police.

As Germany's jails and prison camps began to fill with political prisoners, the Nazis developed a system of concentration camps. Small-scale jails in basements and warehouses were transformed into sprawling camps. The camps not only held political enemies of the Nazis. Anyone thought to weaken the Aryan race could be imprisoned. Little by little, Jews, Roma, gays, the mentally ill, the disabled, and others disappeared into the camps. Many of them never saw their freedom again.

Heinrich Himmler, as head of both the Gestapo and the SS, oversaw the concentration camps. Himmler disarmed people with mild-mannered charm. But he ruthlessly carried out Hitler's racist policies and hunted down dissenters. He would eventually transform his terrifying network of camps into a killing ground for more than 11 million people.

CHAPTER 9

On the March Again

Hitler risks war with
France and Britain—
AND GETS AWAY WITH IT.

IN MARCH 1935, ADOLF HITLER TORE UP
the treaty that followed the German surrender after
World War I. He had Joseph Goebbels announce to
a room full of reporters that Germany was rearming.
German generals had been secretly rebuilding the
military since the Nazi takeover. Now Goebbels
proudly told the world: Germany would have an army

of 300,000 men—three times larger than the Treaty of Versailles allowed.

With the defiant announcement, Hitler risked provoking war with Great Britain and France. But neither country had the stomach for a fight. The wounds of World War I were still too fresh, and no one wanted to fight a costly war during a global depression. French and British foreign ministers responded with little more than weak protests.

Hitler had gambled and won.

Now that Germany could rearm openly, the stalled economy cranked into motion. Factories hummed as they churned out airplanes and tanks. Long-idle shipyards crawled with busy workers. Millions of unemployed laborers returned to work.

Emboldened by his success, Hitler decided to challenge another restriction from the World War I settlement. Since 1919, Germany had been barred from building fortifications near the Rhine River, along the border with France. This 50-mile-wide "demilitarized zone" in the Rhineland had been created to prevent another German invasion of France.

On March 7, 1936, Hitler sent 30,000 soldiers marching into the Rhineland in complete disregard of the treaty. They had orders to pull back immediately if French troops mobilized to stop them.

GERMAN CAVALRY are welcomed with flowers after reoccupying the Rhineland region in March 1936. For the first time since World War I, Germany had soldiers menacing the border with France.

The French prime minister, Albert Sarraut, had a chance to hand Hitler an embarrassing defeat. Sarraut declared that there could be no peace in Europe if Hitler's act were allowed to stand. But in the end he backed down, and French troops stayed in their barracks.

Hitler had triumphed again. Now he could boast that he had restored the pride of Germany, nearly two decades after its surrender in World War I. "We have sovereignty again over our own land," he crowed.

Most Germans rejoiced in the reoccupation of the Rhineland. They cheered as they watched newsreels of Rhinelanders throwing flowers to German troops. Crowds applauded Hitler whenever he appeared in public.

But the Rhineland was only the beginning of Hitler's plans for German expansion. He already had an eye on lands beyond Germany's borders.

CHAPTER 10

First Conquests

THE NAZI MENACE begins
to spread beyond the borders
of Germany.

AFTER MARCHING INTO THE RHINELAND,
Hitler began to fan the flames of German nationalism.
Millions of German-speaking people lived outside
the borders of Germany—in Austria and in the
Sudetenland region of Czechoslovakia. Hitler was
obsessed with making these areas part of Germany.
"One blood demands one Reich!" he had insisted in the
pages of *Mein Kampf*.

Austria became the first target. Germany's neighbor to the south already had an active Nazi Party. For several years, Austrian Nazis had been demanding that Austria become a part of Germany. Austria's chancellor, Kurt Schuschnigg, had firmly refused. Austria was a sovereign nation and most of its people did not want to be dominated by Hitler's regime.

On February 12, 1938, Hitler summoned Schuschnigg to the Berghof, his house in the German Alps. When Schuschnigg arrived, he politely complimented Hitler on the breathtaking view from his large picture window. Hitler replied by launching into a rant that lasted for hours. He insisted that Schuschnigg hand over power to the Austrian Nazis. When Schuschnigg refused, Hitler warned that the Germans could invade Austria at any moment. "Perhaps you will wake up one morning in Vienna to find us there—just like a spring storm," Hitler shouted. "And then you'll see something!"

Exactly a month later, Hitler made good on his threat. German troops marched into Austria. Austrian

Nazis seized important government offices in Vienna, and Schuschnigg was forced to resign. Crowds of Nazi supporters jammed the roads to greet the German soldiers. When Hitler arrived by motorcade, girls threw flowers at his car. "It is fate," he boasted to an aide. "I am destined to be the führer who will bring all Germans into the Greater German Reich."

Shortly after the celebration, Austria's Jewish population felt the racist rage of their new rulers. Austrian Nazis invaded Jewish neighborhoods looking for people to assault or arrest. They forced elderly Jews to scrub old political slogans off the walls with toothbrushes. In one city park, a gang of thugs made a group of Jews eat grass while crowds jeered.

One survivor was horrified by a scene that took place outside his apartment building. "I craned my neck," he said, "and saw an Austrian policeman, a swastika armband already over his dark green uniform sleeve, his truncheon in his fist, lashing out with berserk fury at a man writhing at his feet. I immediately recognized that policeman. I had known him all my life."

A dark cloud had begun to spread across Europe, and its shadow was about to fall on another of Germany's

AUSTRIAN NAZIS watch as Jews are forced to scrub a Vienna sidewalk. After the Germans annexed Austria in March 1938, Austrian Nazis were given free reign to persecute Jews.

neighbors. Czechoslovakia was home to 3.5 million German-speaking people living in the Sudetenland region, which bordered Germany. Emboldened by his seizure of Austria, Hitler began to demand control over the Sudetenland.

When Czech leaders refused, Hitler sent troops to the border. He threatened to invade if the Czechs did not hand over the Sudetenland by October 1.

Suddenly, Europe stood on the verge of war. If the German army invaded, Britain and France might decide to defend Czechoslovakia. Hitler did not seem to care. "Long live war," he blustered to a Sudeten German leader, "even if it lasts from two to eight years."

Faced with Hitler's belligerence, the British and the French backed down. Both countries had struggled to come out of the Great Depression and were unprepared for war with a rearmed, aggressive Germany. Instead of risking a bloody clash with the German army, they gave Hitler what he wanted—a policy that became known as "appeasement."

During the last days of September, British Prime Minister Neville Chamberlain and French Prime Minister Édouard Daladier met with Hitler in Munich. The Czechs were not invited. At the Munich Conference, Chamberlain and Daladier made it clear that they would not help the Czechs defend the Sudetenland.

Deserted by their allies, the Czechs gave up the Sudetenland on the day of the deadline.

When Chamberlain returned from Munich, he was hailed as a hero for saving Britain from war. "I believe it is peace for our time," he boasted.

It would take less than a year for Hitler to prove him wrong.

CHAPTER 11

"This Must Be Hell"

The Nazis persecute German Jews, as Hitler pushes Europe TO THE BRINK OF WAR.

On THE NIGHT OF NOVEMBER 9, 1938, hair-raising howls echoed in the cities of Germany. Hitler's Brownshirts took over the streets, unleashing a long-feared wave of terror on German Jews.

The threat of massive violence had been hanging over Jewish neighborhoods for years. Since 1933, militant Nazis had been eager to fulfill Hitler's promise to rid

Germany of Jews. Hitler had held them back to avoid damaging Germany's reputation abroad.

Now, after victories in Austria and Czechoslovakia, he no longer cared what international leaders thought. He let regional party leaders know that if anti-Jewish riots broke out, they would not be discouraged.

That was all the Nazis needed to hear. SS and SA troops hit the streets armed with sledgehammers and axes. They destroyed Jewish shops and set fire to synagogues and temples. They arrested wealthy Jewish men and beat anyone who tried to resist.

No one even attempted to stop the violence. Crowds gathered in the streets and looked on in silence. Policemen directed traffic and arrested Jews "for their own protection."

After two days of violence, Jewish victims were left to clean up the shards of broken windows and try to rebuild their businesses. Some 7,000 shops and at least 200 synagogues had been destroyed. The German government confiscated one-fifth of the property

BERLINERS PASS BY the shattered windows of a Jewish shop in the aftermath of the Kristallnacht riots on November 9, 1938.

owned by Jews and seized the insurance money on the property that was damaged.

By the time the riots ended, nearly 30,000 people had been arrested and sent to concentration camps. More than 90 people had died in the violence and at least 2,000 more would perish in the camps.

The riots became known as *Kristallnacht*, or the "Night of Broken Glass." One Jewish woman, who was ten years old at the time, remembered standing in the ruins of her neighborhood after the violence ended. "This is what hell is like," she thought. "This must be hell."

Kristallnacht heightened tensions between Germany and the rest of the world. European countries condemned the massacre. U.S. President Franklin Roosevelt protested by withdrawing the American ambassador in Berlin.

But Hitler would not back down. In the months that followed, he kept up the pressure on German Jews, driving them into exile or poverty. He also continued to seize new territory for Germany. On March 15, 1939, German troops took over what was left of Czechoslovakia.

In London, Prime Minister Chamberlain finally realized that Hitler could not be trusted. He vowed that Britain would resist Hitler "to the uttermost of its power." Then he gave his support to the country widely believed to be Hitler's next target. Chamberlain promised to come to Poland's aid if Germany attacked.

When Hitler learned of Chamberlain's promise, he

flew into a rage. "I'll cook [the British] a stew they will choke on!" he screamed.

Hitler spent the summer of 1939 plotting his next steps. In May, he signed an alliance called the "Pact of Steel" with Italy's dictator, Benito Mussolini. Japan would later join the pact, and the three nations became known as the Axis powers.

Hitler's most astonishing move came three months later, when he began negotiations with Soviet leader Joseph Stalin. The Nazis were the sworn enemies of the Soviet Union and its communist government. In *Mein Kampf*, Hitler had outlined his plans to invade the Soviet Union and enslave its people.

But Hitler had more immediate plans, and in order for them to succeed, he needed the Soviets on his side. As Chamberlain had suspected, Hitler wanted to invade Poland. He needed to make sure that the Soviets would not join Britain and France and rush to Poland's aid.

So in August 1939, Hitler asked Stalin for a non-aggression pact between the two countries. The two dictators would agree not to attack each other for ten years. After the German army invaded Poland, Hitler would divide any conquered territory with the Soviet Union.

Stalin agreed to Hitler's terms. The Soviet leader knew that his armies were not ready to face the German war machine. He needed time to strengthen the Red Army before he could consider opposing Germany. And after Britain and France abandoned Czechoslovakia, Stalin concluded that he could not count on them as allies.

When Hitler heard of Stalin's acceptance, he banged his fists on his dining table at the Berghof. "I have them!" he cried. "I have them!"

On the evening of August 24, less than a day after the treaty was signed, Hitler and his entourage watched the Northern Lights from his terrace at the Berghof. The shimmering sky suddenly bathed the group in deep red. "Looks like a great deal of blood," Hitler remarked to an aide. "This time we won't bring it off without violence."

Images from the Holocaust

Spreading Hatred

NAZI MENACE

Hitler became chancellor in 1933. The signs of Nazi rule followed: massive rallies, the swastika flag, the stiff-arm salute, and hate speech against Jews.

CENSORSHIP

Once in power, the Nazis encouraged public displays of anti-Semitism. Here, Hitler Youth burn books condemned as pro-Jewish or pro-communist.

Deutsche!
Wehrt Euch!
Kauft nicht bei Juden!

OUTCASTS

Two Nazis post a sign on a Jewish store in Berlin that says "Don't Buy from Jews!" Nazi laws banned Jews from many occupations.

THE HATRED SPREADS

After Hitler took control of Austria in 1938, Austrian Jews became targets. In this photo, Nazis force Jewish men to scrub a sidewalk in Vienna.

NIGHT OF TERROR

Berliners survey the aftermath of Kristallnacht, a night of anti-Semitic riots that destroyed thousands of Jewish shops in November 1938.

SINGLED OUT

Jews in Germany and Nazi-occupied territories had to carry special identity cards. This one is from Romania in 1942.

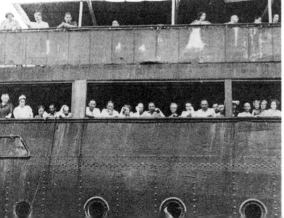

NO ESCAPE

Many Jews tried to flee Nazi Germany. Often they had trouble finding sanctuary. In 1939, more than 900 refugees on this ship were forced back to Europe after being turned away by Cuba and the United States.

MASS MURDER

Hitler salutes German tanks after the conquest of Poland. He had ominously predicted that Jews would be "annihilated" in a world war.

CROWDED INTO GHETTOS
A Nazi guard checks the papers of Jews in the Warsaw ghetto in Poland. In German-occupied areas, Jews were forced into crowded ghettos near rail lines that would later carry them to concentration camps.

IN COLD BLOOD
A German soldier executes a Soviet Jew at the edge of a mass grave. In 1941, special units followed Hitler's invading armies into the Soviet Union with orders to eliminate all Jews.

FINAL DAYS

Early in 1942, Hitler's murderous "Final Solution" was set in motion. Jews from all over Nazi-occupied Europe were loaded into cattle cars and sent to death camps in Poland.

CREMATED

After being gassed, shot, or starved to death, Hitler's victims were cremated in ovens. This photo was taken at Dachau.

RESISTANCE

In 1943, Jewish fighters in the Warsaw ghetto battled the Nazis for almost a month. Survivors of the failed uprising, like those in this photo, were executed or sent to labor camps.

HORRORS REVEALED

A NIGHTMARE ENDS
In April 1945, Allied troops liberated concentration camps in Germany and Eastern Europe. Here, survivors of a German camp are moved to a hospital for treatment.

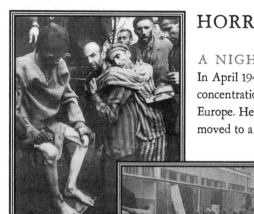

FINAL TOLL
U.S. troops walk past corpses at the Nordhausen concentration camp in Germany. An estimated 11 million victims were murdered in the Nazi camps during the war.

KILLING ROOMS
The walls of this gas chamber at Majdanek in Poland were stained by Zyklon B, a gas used to murder inmates.

HITLER'S LEGACY

The Nazis' victims were stripped of shoes and other personal belongings before being sent to their deaths.

JUSTICE AT LAST

Many Nazi leaders were tried for war crimes. Adolf Eichmann, who organized the deportation of Jews to death camps, was captured in 1960 and sentenced to death for crimes against humanity.

MARKED FOR LIFE

Yaakov Zawadzki (left), Anshel Sieradzki (center), and Menachem Sholowicz show the identification numbers that were tattooed on their arms when they were teenagers at Auschwitz.

PART 3

A DARK CURTAIN OF TERROR

CHAPTER 12

Blitzkrieg

Hitler's armies STUN
THE WORLD by overrunning
most of Europe.

AT 4:40 A.M. ON SEPTEMBER 1, 1939, A FLEET
of Stuka dive bombers began the invasion of Poland.
They resembled birds of prey as they swept down on
Polish cities. Hitler had ordered sirens placed on the
Stuka wings. As the planes dived, spraying bullets and
dropping bombs, the sirens sent out an unearthly wail.
The terrifying sound froze the blood of everyone below.

Just hours after the Stukas broke into Polish
airspace, German armies invaded from the north, south,

STUKA DIVE BOMBERS led the German invasion of Poland in September 1939. The Soviet Union invaded Poland from the east two weeks later.

and west. Some 2,500 tanks led 1.5 million soldiers on a swift and brutal march across Poland. Hitler's *blitzkrieg*, or lightning war, had begun.

Britain and France responded by declaring war on Germany. Appeasement had failed miserably. British Prime Minister Chamberlain was forced to admit that "peace for our time" had been an illusion. Until the Nazis were thrown out of power, he declared, "there will be no peace in Europe."

Little by little, other nations would be drawn into the fight against Germany, Japan, and Italy. Together, these opponents of the Axis powers would become known as the Allies.

For now, however, Britain and France were powerless to help Poland. They could not mobilize and transport troops fast enough to stop the relentless German attack. Then, on September 17, the Soviet Red Army invaded Poland from the east, squeezing the Poles between two hostile forces. After two more weeks of desperate fighting, Polish resistance collapsed. Stalin and Hitler divided Poland between them.

As the smoke cleared over Poland, the world awaited Hitler's next move. Britain and France decided against an invasion of Germany. Instead they would rely on their formidable defenses. Great Britain was an island nation protected by the world's most powerful navy. France sat behind a massive line of fortifications along the German border known as the Maginot Line. The French hoped that Hitler would waste weapons, ammunition, and manpower making fruitless attacks against these forts.

Hitler had no intention of wasting his resources. When he finally launched his attack, it came with blinding speed and brutal violence. The world had never seen warfare like this. The invasions began in April 1940, when German forces overran both Denmark and Norway.

A month later, on May 10, Hitler targeted the Netherlands, Belgium, Luxembourg, and France. The German air force, or *Luftwaffe*, led the way, crippling the tiny air fleets of the Netherlands and Belgium. Paratroopers destroyed bridges and railroads.

Later that day, Hitler's tanks led a massive army into the Netherlands, Luxembourg, and Belgium. The French rushed their most experienced troops north to stop the invasion—exactly as Hitler had hoped.

With French defenses softened, Hitler launched his attack on France. He sent his tanks rolling toward the thick Ardennes forest along the border between France and Belgium. The French had considered the forest to be impassable and left it unguarded by Maginot Line fortresses.

In just three days, the German blitzkrieg shattered all the hopes the French had placed on the Maginot Line. An armored German force led by 2,000 tanks broke through the forest and swept west and north toward the Atlantic coast. The German line now formed a giant arc that squeezed the Allied armies into a rapidly shrinking pocket.

GERMAN TANKS smash through Belgium in May 1940. Hitler's conquest of Western Europe was concluded in less than six weeks.

Just two weeks after the Germans invaded, nearly half a million Allied troops stood trapped against the English Channel in northern France. The British organized a massive evacuation effort. They commandeered a vast fleet of small ships to sail across the channel to Dunkirk, France, and ferry the troops back to Britain. In nine days, fishing boats, yachts, sailing ships, and other vessels rescued more than 330,000 men.

The evacuation at Dunkirk, however, could not save France. On June 21, 1940, Hitler personally accepted the French surrender. He designed the event to humiliate the French leaders. They had to sign away their country's freedom in the same railroad car used for the German surrender at the end of World War I.

"Germany's honor has been restored with this historic act," Hitler declared.

When Hitler returned to Germany, the country celebrated. Shops in Berlin closed at noon. Jubilant crowds lined the streets waving swastika flags. Girls filled the roadside to throw rose petals as Hitler's car drove by.

But in the hundreds of towns and cities that had just fallen to the Nazis, a dark curtain of terror began to fall. Squads of Gestapo agents and SS troops followed closely behind the German army. They tracked down anyone who dared to resist the Nazi occupation forces—often with help from local residents and government officials. Some victims were killed outright. Others were sent to the concentration camps that the Germans were building in Poland and other occupied territories.

As always, Jews bore the brunt of the Nazis' hatred. Gradually, they were separated from the rest of the population. They were forced to wear yellow stars on their clothing so they could be easily identified. Before long, they lost their jobs and their homes.

Anne Frank was ten years old and living in Amsterdam, in the Netherlands, when the Nazis invaded. In her diary, she recorded a long list of activities that gradually became off limits to Jews. She and her friends were forced to stop riding in streetcars and automobiles. They were barred from movies,

IN NAZI-OCCUPIED EUROPE, Jews were singled out from
the rest of the population and sent to labor camps or forced into
crowded ghettos. Like these residents of Lodz, Poland, they were
forced to wear yellow stars that identified them as Jews.

swimming pools, and athletic fields. They were forced
to shop between 3 and 5 P.M. and to stay inside at night.
"I don't dare do anything anymore," a friend said to her,
"because I'm afraid it's not allowed."

As the occupation wore on, SS guards began crowding Jews into cities, where they were forced into filthy, overpopulated ghettos. SS leader Heinrich Himmler made sure that each ghetto was located near a railroad line——so that prisoners could later be transported to concentration camps.

Anne's older sister, Margot, eventually received a "call-up" notice, ordering her to report for duty at a Nazi labor camp. "A call-up: everyone knows what that means," Anne wrote. "Visions of concentration camps and lonely cells raced through my head."

The Franks went into hiding. Their refuge protected them from the Nazis for two years. But Anne, Margot, and their mother eventually died in a Nazi concentration camp. More than 100,000 Dutch Jews—— nearly 80 percent of the Jewish population in the Netherlands——would suffer the same fate before the Nazi occupation finally ended.

IN 1940, NAZIS ORDERED JEWS in and around Warsaw, Poland, to move to this small, walled-off area of the city. The Warsaw ghetto, as it was known, was severely overcrowded. On average, seven people lived in a single room. Within two years, about 83,000 people died of starvation and disease. This photo shows corpses on a street in the ghetto; the ghetto wall is in the background.

CHAPTER 13

Battle for Britain

Hitler's air force tries to COMPLETE
THE CONQUEST of Western Europe.

WITH THE FALL OF FRANCE, HITLER FELT
certain he had won the war in the west. Of the major
Allied powers, only Great Britain had survived the
German assault.

The U.S. supplied Britain with much-needed
weapons and other goods. But the Americans were not
yet willing to join the war against Nazi Germany.

Hitler was convinced that the British would
recognize their isolation and negotiate for peace. Then

he could devote himself to his true goal. He would turn on his Soviet allies, invade Eastern Europe, and expel or slaughter more than 50 million people to make room for German colonists.

The British, however, were no longer in the mood to make peace. Their new prime minister, Winston Churchill, prepared his country for a fight to the death. "We shall defend our island, whatever the cost may be," he announced. "We shall fight on the beaches, we shall fight on the landing grounds, we shall fight in the fields and in the streets, we shall fight in the hills; we shall never surrender."

Faced with Churchill's refusal to negotiate, Hitler set in motion a plan to invade Great Britain. On August 12, 1940, he began a massive air assault to soften British defenses. Night after night, German planes rained bombs on British airfields, factories, and cities. The raids drove Londoners into basements and subway tunnels for protection. More than 1.5 million people, many of them children, were eventually evacuated to the countryside.

AS BOMBS FELL on London during the Battle of Britain, many people took refuge in subway stations. This station is so crowded that people slept on the tracks.

The Battle of Britain, as it was called, raged in the skies for more than two months. The German raids killed more than 20,000 British civilians and reduced thousands of buildings to rubble. But Britain's Royal Air Force (RAF) took its toll on the German Luftwaffe, shooting down nearly 2,000 planes.

In the middle of October, the RAF's heroics forced Hitler to end regular bombing raids. The British had been hit with the full force of the Luftwaffe. They emerged battered but still standing. "We are waiting for the long-promised invasion," Churchill said in a radio address to the nation. "So are the fishes."

Hitler had suffered his first defeat of the war. Yet he casually brushed off the failure. He turned instead to his true obsession, the invasion of the Soviet Union—now code-named Operation Barbarossa.

In December, Hitler began to prepare the German people for his new campaign. In a speech to Berliners, he returned to his obsession with "living space." He claimed that Germany had just one square mile for every 360 people while other nations clung to vast stretches of open land. Despite the fact that Germany had no problem with overcrowding, he insisted that the nation needed to expand its borders. "We must solve these problems, and therefore we will solve them!" he declared.

The following March, Hitler assembled more than 200 of his military commanders to announce a final plan for the attack. He made it clear that the invasion of the Soviet Union would be more than just a military operation. It was a campaign to wipe out communism and subjugate the Jews and Slavs of Eastern Europe. Hitler wanted to expel or exterminate all Jews in the conquered territories. Slavs would be executed, deported, or forced to work as slave laborers for German colonists.

"This struggle is one of ideologies and racial differences, and will have to be conducted with unprecedented, merciless, and unrelenting harshness," Hitler commanded.

If Hitler's military leaders had any objections, they did not voice them. Instead, they went back to their posts and prepared for Operation Barbarossa. By June, all eastbound roads and rail lines in Germany were clogged with traffic. More than three million soldiers took up their places along a 930-mile front and prepared to invade the Soviet Union.

CHAPTER 14

Clash in the East

Hitler turns on a former ally
and SHOWS NO MERCY.

AT 3:15 A.M. ON JUNE 22, 1941, 6,000 GERMAN
artillery guns shattered the stillness along the Soviet
border. Luftwaffe dive bombers screamed out of the sky.
The largest invasion in the history of war had begun.

At his military headquarters, known as the Wolf's
Lair, Hitler listened to battlefield reports with mounting
glee. Soviet dictator Joseph Stalin had ignored warnings
of the impending invasion. His forces were taken
completely by surprise. Dive bombers destroyed entire

airfields before Soviet planes could leave the ground. Ground troops surrounded and slaughtered entire divisions of the Red Army. According to one report, a group of German motorcyclists fell upon surprised Red Army recruits in the middle of their basic training.

The disorganized Red Army could not stop the German blitzkrieg. By September, German armies had advanced 400 miles into the Soviet Union along a 1,000-mile front. Leningrad was nearly surrounded, and 2,000 German tanks were closing in on Moscow, the Soviet capital. On October 2, Hitler announced that the Soviets had lost 2.5 million men, 18,000 tanks, and 14,500 planes. The enemy, Hitler declared, was "already beaten and would never rise again!"

Attempting to make Hitler's prediction come true, Nazi commanders showed no mercy to the Soviet people. Behind the army traveled special SS police units called *Einsatzgruppen*—task groups. They rounded up Communist Party leaders and Jews. Prisoners were lined up and executed or deported to concentration camps.

One task group of 500 men killed at least 90,000 Soviets in the first year alone.

Instead of crushing Soviet resistance, Hitler's cruelty helped to turn a beaten people into fierce opponents. The Soviet people had suffered under their own dictator, Stalin, and many of them wanted to welcome the Germans as liberators. But as word of the atrocities spread, civilian resistance to the Germans stiffened. People who might have cooperated with the invaders instead took up arms against them by the thousands.

In November, Soviet troops began to make a stand in the suburbs of Moscow. And there, the blitzkrieg began to stall. The Germans had planned for a quick victory, a gamble that had paid off in Poland and France. They were unprepared to fight a long campaign in the east while the war with Britain continued in the west.

The Russian winter added to Hitler's problems, and the German assault froze in place. Hitler's men could see the spires of Moscow, but they could move no farther. Tank engines refused to start. Planes could

GERMAN SOLDIERS execute a group of Soviet civilians
during the early days of Operation Barbarossa. Hitler had ordered
his troops to wage a war of "extinction."

not get off the ground. Supply trains got stuck in the
snow. To make matters worse, Hitler had failed to
provide warm clothing for his men. He had expected
the campaign to be over before winter.

Condemned by their führer's arrogance, German
troops suffered in the cold. Lightly clad men froze to
death. Some were crippled by frostbite. Still others
grew weak from malnutrition as food supplies ran low.
Hitler's generals begged him to retreat and regroup. He
refused to give up an inch of conquered ground.

At this point, Stalin unleashed a surprise of his own. A Soviet counterattack pushed the invaders back 150 miles before the Germans dug in and held the line.

While the German armies battled in the east, Hitler's war took another fateful turn. On December 7, 1941, an aide burst into the führer's office. He announced that the Japanese had launched a surprise attack on the U.S. naval base at Pearl Harbor, Hawaii.

Hitler was stunned. Here was a development that could change the course of the war. Japan, with its powerful navy, would become a full-fledged ally. Yet the United States would now commit the full weight of its combat forces to the battle against the Axis powers.

Hitler wanted to join the Japanese and declare war on the United States immediately. Aides urged him to let the U.S. be the aggressor. But Hitler was eager for a chance to punish the Americans for their support of Britain. On December 11, he announced to the world that he was going to war against the United States. "We will always strike first!" he declared.

CHAPTER 15

Holocaust

Hitler sets in motion his war
of EXTERMINATION against
the Jews of Europe.

ON JANUARY 20, 1942, NAZI LEADERS FROM
Germany and the occupied territories gathered in the
Berlin suburb of Wannsee. The 15 men had been invited
to a conference with an ominous but vague-sounding
subject—the "final solution of the Jewish question."

For years Hitler had been elusive about his exact
plans for an assault on the Jewish population of Europe.
Nazi leaders had discussed deporting Jews to Siberia

or Madagascar. But German troops had not secured enough territory. With that option gone, the "Final Solution" began to take a new shape. It was a plan of almost unimaginable scope and cruelty—the systematic murder, or genocide, of all the Jews in Europe.

At the Wannsee Conference, the new plan was set in motion. The meeting was led by SS chief Himmler's second-in-command, Reinhard Heydrich. He gave the 15 attendees clear instructions. There were nine million Jews living in territory occupied or invaded by the Germany army, he claimed. He wanted them all shipped to railroad centers, crammed into boxcars, and deported to concentration camps in Poland. At the camps, they would be forced to work until they died. Those who survived would be eliminated by other means.

Himmler had already asked the chief physician of the SS for advice on how to carry out Hitler's diabolical plan. The physician suggested killing prisoners in chambers filled with poison gas. One such gas chamber had been tested on September 3, 1941, at the Auschwitz

HUNGARIAN JEWS arrive at the Auschwitz extermination camp in German-occupied Poland in June 1944. More than 400,000 Jews from Hungary alone were murdered in Auschwitz.

camp in Poland. Some 850 Russian and Polish inmates were forced into a basement cell that day and murdered with Zyklon B, a poison gas.

After the Wannsee Conference, five new extermination camps were built, and a horrifying process began at each one. Boxcars loaded with terrified prisoners arrived at their gates. At Auschwitz, the largest of the camps, trains arrived daily bearing an average of 1,000 inmates. Guards separated the new arrivals into two groups: those who were strong enough to work and those who were not.

Those in the first group were lined up and tattooed with identification numbers. People in the second group were led into a chamber disguised as a shower room and gassed to death. When the gas cleared, guards removed gold teeth and anything else of value from the bodies. Then the corpses were cremated in huge ovens.

Samuel Willenberg, a young Polish Jew, miraculously survived the extermination camp known as Treblinka. He said the Nazis hid the real purpose of the camp from outsiders and prisoners. The stunned, starving new arrivals assumed that they were being sent to showers. Most people could not comprehend that the camp was set up just to kill them. "It was hard to believe," he said. "I was there and still I could not believe it at first."

The extermination camps carried out their horrific mission on a shockingly massive scale. Guards could murder and cremate new arrivals within two hours. Auschwitz was capable of killing 20,000 prisoners a day.

VICTIMS of Hitler's gas chambers were cremated in ovens like these. This photo was taken at Buchenwald after the war.

Elie Wiesel, a 15-year-old Jewish boy from Romania, saw the end result of the slaughter at Auschwitz. "Not far from us, flames were leaping from a ditch, gigantic flames," Wiesel later wrote in his heartbreaking memoir, *Night*. "They were burning something. A lorry drew up at the pit and delivered its load—little children! Babies!"

Wiesel's book, and the testimony of other survivors, would eventually expose the horrors of the camps to the world. But in 1942, millions of inmates suffered and died in isolation. "Quietly, people asked each other— why? Why?" Samuel Willenberg recalled. "There was no answer."

THE DEAD BODY OF A PRISONER lies
tangled in a barbed-wire fence at Auschwitz.

CHAPTER 16

Turning Points

The TIDE OF THE WAR
TURNS against Hitler at
El Alamein and Stalingrad.

BY THE MIDDLE OF 1942, HITLER KNEW
the war had reached a critical phase. The United States
and the Soviet Union had greater resources and greater
manpower than Germany. Hitler would have to crush
the Allies quickly or they would overwhelm him.

But two epic defeats destroyed Hitler's hope for
a quick victory. The first occurred in North Africa,
where Axis troops had been fighting the Allies since
September 1940. The two sides had waged massive

tank battles, pushing the lines of battle back and forth across the desert sands. At stake were waterways that controlled access to the vast oil fields of the Middle East.

In early November, the Allies took firm control of the desert war. During a two-week battle at El Alamein, Egypt, the British devastated the army of German Field

A GERMAN soldier surrenders to a British rifleman at El Alamein, a desert tank battle that turned the tide of the war in North Africa.

Marshal Erwin Rommel. Rommel begged Hitler to allow his mauled forces to retreat to Europe. True to form, Hitler insisted that Rommel stay in Africa at all costs. Rommel fled westward across the desert with the British general, Bernard Montgomery, chasing him. Then American troops landed on the shores of Algeria and Morocco and began moving east. Rommel was trapped.

The second, more devastating blow came on the Eastern Front, at the Soviet city of Stalingrad. In June 1942, Hitler had launched a new offensive in southern Russia. At first, the attack moved as quickly as previous blitzkriegs. But the German Sixth Army stalled at the city of Stalingrad, where Stalin had decided to make a stand.

Fighting raged in Stalingrad throughout the fall. German bombs turned most of the city to rubble and ash. But the Soviets fought back fiercely. Their fighter planes shot down half the bombers the Germans put in the sky. And the Germans had to measure ground gained by the yard.

Early in November, German commander General Friedrich Paulus realized that the offensive was going nowhere. He noticed Soviet tanks arriving in force to the north and asked Hitler for permission to retreat.

The führer refused, sealing the fate of hundreds of thousands of German soldiers.

On November 22, the Red Army launched a massive counterattack. Within hours, more than 200,000 of Paulus's men were surrounded.

Each day Hitler received updates on the desperate plight of his soldiers in Stalingrad. Frozen and hungry, Paulus's soldiers were bombarded again and again by Soviet artillery. Paulus requested permission to surrender. Hitler radioed back: "I will not freely give up Stalingrad, even if the whole Sixth Army perishes in the act!"

On January 31, 1943, Paulus ignored the führer's orders and surrendered along with the last 91,000 of his soldiers. When Hitler heard the news, he flew into a rage. The defenders should have "shot themselves with their last bullets," he fumed.

GERMAN PRISONERS are led away after their defeat at
Stalingrad. The German Sixth Army was destroyed during
the brutal four-month battle.

Finally, when he finished his tirade, Hitler became
despondent. "I need a million new soldiers," he sighed.

By 1943, however, the German people were exhausted. To recruit new soldiers, Hitler had to pull workers from important war industries. And civilian morale was suffering. Food and other consumer goods were severely rationed. Urban areas endured relentless pounding from U.S. and British bombers. Once-beautiful cities like Hamburg and Berlin became wastelands. All the necessities of life disappeared. "There was no water, no light, no fire," one witness recalled.

Throughout the year, the Allies struck one blow after another against the German army. In the summer, the Red Army destroyed a German tank force near Kursk in the Soviet Union. It was the largest tank battle ever fought. When it was over, the husks of 900 crippled tanks littered the battlefield. The Germans began a long retreat from their führer's brutal war of annihilation in the east.

As the Germans reeled from the disaster on the Eastern Front, nearly half a million U.S. and British troops stormed the shores of Sicily, just off the Italian mainland. With Mussolini's government crumbling, his opponents overthrew him. Italy's new government sided with the Allies.

In Berlin, Hitler began to fall apart from the stress of failure. He endured stomach cramps and panic attacks. One moment his collar was too tight and he couldn't breath. The next moment his skin itched. He scratched his neck and ears until they bled. He chewed his fingernails. Doctors kept him on a steady stream of drugs to relieve his anxiety and his pain. He took heavy doses of sleeping pills every night.

The führer, who had once declared himself "more godlike than human," now seemed to be nearing his mortal end.

Chapter 17

End of a Nightmare

His Nazi dream in ruins, Hitler
faces the final days of his
MURDEROUS REIGN.

Under a gray dawn sky on the morning of June 6, 1944—known as D-Day to the Allies—the first of 160,000 U.S., British, and Canadian troops waded ashore in Nazi-occupied France. They scrambled up the beaches under heavy fire and began the long-awaited liberation of Western Europe.

Within a month, one million Allied soldiers and a vast train of supplies had landed in France. In fierce fighting, they began to push the Nazis out of the land they had conquered during the blitzkrieg of June 1940. They liberated Paris in August and Brussels, Belgium, in September. In November, they broke across Germany's western border in vast numbers.

Meanwhile, the Red Army closed relentlessly in from the east. They fought through Poland and reached the border of Germany at the end of January 1945.

Hitler's fanatical crusade to dominate Europe had finally been crushed. As his plans collapsed around him, Hitler became increasingly paranoid. He believed that someone was trying to poison his soap, his toothpaste, his shaving cream. He insisted that his aides check and double-check everything he consumed.

In April, the Soviets surrounded Berlin. Hitler's supporters begged him to flee the capital, but he refused. He retreated to the "führer bunker," a bombproof maze of 16 rooms 33 feet below his offices. Each small room was lit by a single naked light bulb. Noisy diesel generators kept the lights running and circulated air.

Hitler shared the bunker with a gathering of generals, top aides, servants, and secretaries. The moist air hung heavy with diesel fumes and the smell of sweat. Though Hitler had banned cigarettes, many of his followers now smoked openly.

From these dim quarters, Hitler oversaw the final days of the war. His mood swung from despair to fits of crazed optimism. He barked at his generals to attack with armies that had been destroyed long ago. If they protested, he shouted them down.

When he finally admitted that the war was lost, he ordered his generals to destroy Germany. Everything valuable was to be blown up or leveled—cities, factories, bridges, museums, and farms. Hitler wanted nothing left to the invaders.

As always, he refused to accept responsibility for the catastrophe he had caused. He had been betrayed by Germany's weakness, he insisted. "If the German people lose this war," he yelled, "they will have proved themselves unworthy of me!"

A DEFEATED GERMAN soldier sits beside the ruins of the Reichstag after learning that Germany had surrendered to the Allies.

Above the bunker, Berlin lay in smoking ruins. Soviet artillery demolished buildings and destroyed roads. Sirens wailed at all hours to announce air attacks. Fires raged uncontrolled. Bodies and burned-out vehicles littered the streets. Animals from the city zoo wandered through the rubble.

On April 29, Hitler married his longtime girlfriend, Eva Braun. Then he called in a secretary and dictated his final will and testament. In it he vented his hatred for the Jewish people one last time.

The following day, Hitler and Braun entered the führer's study with two pistols and two capsules of cyanide poison. The dull roar of the diesel generator made it hard for those outside the room to hear. At about 3:30 P.M., one of Hitler's attendants smelled gun smoke. He and two others cautiously entered the room.

The man who had imposed a reign of terror on most of Europe was dead. Both Hitler and his wife had swallowed their cyanide capsules. Hitler had shot himself in the temple to make sure the job was done.

One of the attendants emerged from the room and faced the expectant crowd that had gathered. He clicked his heels in military fashion and announced, "I must report: The führer is dead!"

HITLER'S BUNKER in Berlin, where he committed suicide. His body was dissected by Soviet doctors. His skull was shipped to Moscow.

Epilogue

Hitler's war ended eight days after his death. On May 8, 1945, Germany surrendered to the Allies. The war in the Pacific continued until Japan surrendered on August 15.

The six years of World War II were the most destructive in history. An estimated 60 million people died, two-thirds of them civilians. At least 11 million inmates perished in Hitler's concentration camps, including six million Jews. They were victims of the most extensive campaign of systematic murder the world has ever known.

As the Allies advanced on Germany at the end of the war, they discovered the evidence of Hitler's great crime against the Jews of Europe—known today as the Holocaust. They liberated camps such as Dachau and Buchenwald, whose horrors Edward R. Murrow struggled to describe to his radio audience. They uncovered mass graves, some containing thousands of bodies. At Auschwitz in Poland, they found evidence of more than one million murders. The Nazis had slaughtered well over half the Jewish population in the territories they controlled.

With the liberation of these camps, hundreds of thousands of survivors were given a chance to rebuild their shattered lives. Over time, many of them found the strength to tell their stories.

Elie Wiesel, the boy who witnessed bodies burning at Auschwitz, needed ten years to find the words to express his ordeal. The memoir he produced, *Night*, has educated generations of people about the Holocaust. Wiesel says he gets 100 letters a month from children who have been moved by his book.

Many of the people responsible for the Holocaust were punished for their crimes. Joseph Goebbels, Hitler's propaganda minister, committed suicide the day after Hitler did. Heinrich Himmler, the SS commander who oversaw the murder of more than 11 million people, killed himself after surrendering to the Allies.

Just after the war, the Allies held war-crimes trials in Nuremberg, Germany. Nearly 2,000 Nazi officials were eventually tried. Many of them were sentenced to death or to life in prison.

Adolf Hitler, whose hateful vision created the Holocaust, escaped a public trial by taking his own life. But his name remains almost synonymous with evil. His reign was probably the bloodiest of the twentieth century. He came close to imposing his racist nightmare on an entire continent, and perhaps the rest of the world as well.

Since Hitler's death, parts of the world have suffered through the horrors of genocide. But no genocide has been allowed to spread as far as Hitler's. Hopefully the memory of his atrocities will help keep the world from ever again plunging into what Winston Churchill called "the abyss of a new dark age."

GERMAN SOLDIERS hold Jewish women and children prisoner in Warsaw in 1943. The Nazis murdered more than 90 percent of Poland's Jewish population.

TIMELINE OF TERROR

1889

April 20, 1889: Hitler is born.

1919: Hitler joins the Nazi Party and builds a following in Munich.

1924: Hitler writes his autobiography, *Mein Kampf*, while in prison.

1934: Hitler dismantles legal freedoms in Germany and declares himself dictator.

1936–1938: Hitler rearms Germany and seizes Austria and Czechoslovakia.

September 1, 1939: World War II begins with Germany's invasion of Poland.

June 1941: Hitler invades the Soviet Union.

December 1941: The U.S. joins the Allies and enters the war.

June 6, 1944: The Allied invasion of Nazi-occupied France begins with the D-Day landings.

1918: After fighting in World War I, Hitler is devastated by Germany's surrender.

1923: The Nazis attempt to seize power in Germany in the failed Beer Hall Putsch.

1933: Hitler becomes chancellor of Germany after leading the Nazi Party to power in democratic elections.

September 1935: The Nuremberg laws strip German Jews of their citizenship.

November 9–11, 1938: Nazi Brownshirts carry out the Kristallnacht assault on German Jews.

May–June 1940: German troop overrun France, Belgium, and the Netherlands, subjecting most of West Europe to Hitler's control.

July–Oct. 1941: The British ai force defeats the German Luftwaffe i the Battle of Britain, foiling German plans for an invasion of Britain.

January 1943: German troop surrender at Stalingrad. German armies begin their final retreat on the Eastern Front.

April 30, 1945: With Soviet troops in Berlin, Hitler commits suicide.

1945

annihilation (uh-nye-uh-LAY-shun) *noun* complete destruction

anti-Semitism (AN-tye-SEM-ih-tiz-uhm) *noun* hostility directed toward Jewish people

appeasement (uh-PEEZ-ment) *noun* a foreign policy strategy of giving into demands in hope of avoiding war

armistice (ARM-iss-tiss) *noun* an agreement to temporarily stop fighting a war

artillery (ar-TIL-uh-ree) *noun* large, crew-operated guns such as cannons and mortars

atrocities (uh-TROSS-uh-teez) *noun* cruel acts, often involving torture or murder

blitzkrieg (BLITZ-kreeg) *noun* an intense military campaign intended to bring about a swift victory; *blitzkrieg* is German for "lightning war"

chancellor (CHAN-suh-lur) *noun* the name for the head of Germany's government since 1871. Like many other parliamentary governments, Germany has both a head of government (chancellor) and a ceremonial head of state (president).

communist (KOM-yuh-nist) *noun* a person who supports communism, a system in which all property belongs to the government and the wealth is shared by all

concentration camp (kon-suhn-TRAY-shun KAMP) *noun* a place in which large numbers of people are imprisoned under extremely harsh conditions to provide forced labor or to await mass execution

conservative (kuhn-SUR-vuh-tiv) *noun* in Germany during the early 1900s, a person who opposed democracy and wanted to reinstate the monarchy

demilitarized zone (dee-MIL-ih-tur-ized ZONE) *noun* a neutral area between rival nations where military activity is not permitted

democratic (dem-uh-KRAH-tik) *adjective* describing a system of government in which the people hold the power, either directly or by voting to elect representatives

deport (dee-PORT) *verb* to expel someone from a country

dissenter (di-SEN-tuhr) *noun* a person who disagrees with an idea or opinion

fanatical (fuh-NAT-ih-kuhl) *adjective* wildly enthusiastic about a belief or cause

führer (FYUR-uhr) *noun* the title that Hitler granted himself when he became chancellor of Germany; *führer* means "leader"

gallows (GAL-ohz) *noun* a wooden frame used to execute people by hanging

genocide (JEN-oh-side) *noun* the systematic killing of an ethnic group

Gestapo (geh-SHTOP-oh) *noun* the German secret police under Nazi rule

ideology (eye-DEE-ol-uh-gee) *noun* the combination of political beliefs that makes up a person's worldview

liberation (lib-uh-RAY-shun) *noun* the act of setting free

Nazi Party (NOT-see PAR-tee) *noun* the political party led by Adolf Hitler that ruled Germany from 1933 to 1945. The Nazis attempted to rid the world of people they considered inferior by murdering millions of Jews, Roma, and others.

newsreel (NOOS-reel) *noun* a short news film shown in movie theaters

ominous (OM-uh-nuhss) *adjective* signaling a coming evil

parliament (PAR-luh-muhnt) *noun* an assembly of elected representatives who make the laws in some countries

propaganda (prop-uh-GAN-duh) *noun* biased information that is spread to influence the way people think

putsch (PUTSCH) *noun* a violent attempt to overthrow a government

Reich (RIKE) *noun* the name for one of the three German empires. The First Reich, also known as the Holy Roman Empire, existed from 926 to 1806. The Second Reich collapsed at the end of World War I. Hitler vowed that his Third Reich would rule for a thousand years.

Reichstag (RIKES-tahg) *noun* the parliament of Germany from 1871 to 1945; also, the building where it met

Roma (ROH-muh) *noun* members of the Romani, an ethnic group that entered Eastern Europe from India more than 500 years ago

sanctuary (SANGK-choo-er-ee) *noun* safety or protection

Schutzstaffel (SS) (SHUTZ-staf-ful) *noun* German for "defense unit." The SS was formed to guard Hitler, but it grew into a huge force that carried out the murder of millions during the Holocaust. SS troops were often called "Blackshirts."

Slav (SLAHV) *noun* a member of an ethnic group that arose in Eastern Europe more than 2,000 years ago. Poles, Russians, Czechs, and other Slavic people speak related languages.

Sturmabteilung (SA) (SHTURM-ab-tye-luhng) *noun* German for "storm detachment." The SA was the Nazi Party's private army, and it helped Hitler rise to power in the 1920s and early 1930s. SA troops were often called "Brownshirts."

swastika (SWAHSS-tuh-kuh) *noun* an ancient symbol consisting of a cross with the arms bent at right angles; it was adopted as the emblem of the Nazi Party

FIND OUT MORE

Here are some books and websites with more information about Adolf Hitler and his times.

BOOKS

Adams, Simon. **World War II (DK Eyewitness Books)**. New York: DK Publishing, 2007. (72 pages) *This richly illustrated book is crammed with photographs, documents, artifacts, and maps.*

Frank, Anne. **The Diary of a Young Girl**. New York: Doubleday, 1995. (340 pages) *This beautifully written diary documents the experiences of a young Jewish girl hiding from the Nazis during World War II.*

Levine, Karen. **Hana's Suitcase: A True Story**. Morton Grove, IL: Albert Whitman & Company, 2003. (111 pages) *A group of schoolchildren in Japan trace the history of a small suitcase to uncover the story of Hana Brady, a child killed at Auschwitz.*

Rice, Earle Jr. **Adolf Hitler and Nazi Germany (World Leaders)**. Greensboro, NC: Morgan Reynolds Publishing, 2005. (176 pages) *A clear, concisely written book about Hitler and his times.*

Wiesel, Elie. **Night**. New York: Hill and Wang, 2006. (120 pages) *Wiesel's powerful memoir of his battle for survival during the Holocaust.*

Wood, Angela Gluck. **Holocaust**. New York, DK Publishing, 2007. (192 pages) *A compelling pictorial overview of the Holocaust.*

WEBSITES

http://london.iwm.org.uk *The website of Britain's Imperial War Museum has a wealth of information about World War II.*

http://www.fordham.edu/halsall/mod/modsbook.html *Fordham University's Internet Modern History Sourcebook includes links to primary-source materials on Nazism, the Holocaust, and World War II.*

http://www.pbs.org/behindcloseddoors *The online companion to the PBS series* World War II: Behind Closed Doors *includes a profile of Hitler and explores Germany's relationship with the Soviet Union during World War II.*

http://www.pbs.org/wgbh/amex/goebbels/peopleevents/p_hitler.html *This online companion to the PBS film* The Man Behind Hitler *focuses on Joseph Goebbels, whose skillful propaganda campaign helped bring the Nazis to power.*

http://www.pbs.org/wgbh/amex/holocaust/index.html *The online companion to the PBS film* America and the Holocaust, *which probes the United States' complex response to the Holocaust.*

http://www.ushmm.org *The website of the United States Holocaust Memorial Museum in Washington, D.C., is one of the best resources on the Web for information about the Holocaust.*

INDEX

Author's Note and Bibliography

As a U.S. soldier in World War II, my father suffered a curious wound. A German soldier shot him and hit a hand grenade hanging on his chest. Thankfully, the grenade did not explode. But the force of the bullet caused it to shatter, sending thousands of pieces of shrapnel into Dad's chest and left arm. In middle age, my father liked to tell his wide-eyed son how little pieces of metal still worked their way to the surface of his arm where he could pull them out.

That hooked me for good on the subject of Hitler and the Nazis. My childhood geography of the world consisted of Texas, where I grew up, and Nazi Germany, where Dad fought. My knowledge has since become a bit more sophisticated. Yet in writing this book I felt very much like that wide-eyed kid again, in awe of the wounds one war can create and how they never altogether heal.

The following sources have been most helpful in researching this book:

Brendon, Piers. **The Dark Valley: A Panorama of the 1930s.** New York: First Vintage, 2000.

Eberle, Henrik and Matthias Uhl. **The Hitler Book: The Secret Dossier Prepared for Stalin from the Interrogations of Hitler's Personal Aides.** New York: PublicAffairs, 2005.

Fest, Joachim C. **Hitler.** New York: Harcourt Brace, 1973.

Hauner, Milan. **Hitler: A Chronology of his Life and Times.** New York: Macmillan Press, 1983.

Heiden, Konrad. **The Fuehrer.** New York: Castle Books, 2002.

Hitler, Adolf. **Mein Kampf.** New York: Houghton Mifflin, 1971.

Kershaw, Ian. **Hitler, 1889–1936: Hubris.** New York: W.W. Norton, 1998.

Kershaw, Ian. **Hitler, 1936–1945: Nemesis.** New York: W.W. Norton, 2000.

Metcalfe, Philip. **1933.** New York: Harper & Row, 1988.

Shirer, William L. **The Rise and Fall of the Third Reich.** New York: Simon and Schuster, 1960.

Stein, George H., ed. **Great Lives Observed: Hitler.** Englewood Cliffs, NJ: Prentice-Hall, 1968.

Toland, John. **Adolf Hitler.** New York: Doubleday & Co., 1976.

—Sean Stewart Price